Thoughts on Children

Thoughts on Children

Johann Christoph Blumhardt
Christoph Friedrich Blumhardt

Plough Publishing House

Published by Plough Publishing House
Rifton, New York
Robertsbridge, England
www.plough.com

First Edition: 1980
Second Edition: 2005

The material in this book has been translated from the German, compiled from various sources. For bibliographic details, see the endnotes.

Front cover image: *Interior with Women and a Child* [detail] (oil on canvas), Mathey, Paul (1844–1929) / Musee d'Orsay, Paris, France / Giraudon / The Bridgeman Art Library

Library of Congress Cataloging-in-Publication Data

Blumhardt, Johann Christoph, 1805-1880.
  Thoughts on children / Johann Christoph Blumhardt, Christoph Friedrich Blumhardt. -- 2nd ed.
      p. cm.
  Originally published: Thoughts on children. 2nd ed. Rifton, N.Y. : Plough ; Robertsbridge, Sussex : Bruderhof Communities on the UK, 2005.
  Includes bibliographical references.
  ISBN 978-0-87486-934-7
  1. Child rearing--Religious aspects--Christianity. 2. Child rearing--Miscellanea. 3. Child psychology--Miscellanea. I. Blumhardt, Christoph, 1842-1919. II. Bruderhof Communities Church International. III. Title.
  HQ772.B5513 2013
  649'.1--dc23
                              2012041608

Contents

Foreword

It is sometimes said that each child is a thought in the mind of God. But even if we believe this, and approach the children entrusted to us with the reverence that such a belief ought to instill, we may often feel helpless – whether in the face of a two-year-old's tantrum, or a teenager's silence.

In this little book, two fathers (themselves a father and son) share their thoughts on the essence of bringing up children. Both lived in Germany in an era when parents and teachers tended to be overly strict, and we live in a time when they tend to be very lenient. All the same, there is plenty in what they say that is timeless.

Johann Christoph Blumhardt (1805–1880) studied theology in Tübingen and became a pastor. He longed to experience the reality of

God, and this he did in a very concrete way when
he dared to take up an intense two-year battle
(1842–44) with the demonic powers that possessed
a tormented woman in his congregation at
Möttlingen. As in New Testament times, demons
were driven out, and the woman was cured. And
all over Germany, Möttlingen became known for
the motto that expressed its inhabitants' joy: Jesus
is victor!

In the following months, a movement of repentance and conversion spread far beyond his parish,
and many other people were healed of physical
illnesses. So many came to him that in 1852 he felt
he had to leave Möttlingen, where he had worked
with his wife for fourteen years (1838–1852), and
move to the large and imposing spa at Bad Boll.
As housefather there, he was able to continue his
growing work of caring for the thousands that
came to him – sick, wounded, and sin-laden souls.

In 1920 A. Albers, a writer for a well-known
publishing house, described the father Blumhardt's
life in these few telling words:

The atmosphere in which this Swabian pastor lived with unwavering certainty was that of early Christianity and the expectation of the final breaking in of the kingdom of God. This is where he drew his strength. In this atmosphere he helped the people of Möttlingen and Bad Boll, who turned to him day and night. His life was one uninterrupted exercise of the powers of love. Here was a man who had a part in what God was doing and who was an instrument in his hands.[1]

Johann Christoph Blumhardt's son Christoph Friedrich (1842–1919) was raised in this atmosphere of expectation and the reality of the presence of God. He too studied theology at Tübingen, and then returned to Bad Boll in 1869 to help his father. In 1880 the elder Blumhardt died, and his son carried on his father's pastorate with similar gifts. He followed so truly in his father's footsteps that the witness they gave to Jesus and the kingdom of God was one and the same.

Christoph Friedrich saw that Christians were turning the biblical expectation of God's kingdom on this earth into a waiting for their personal reward in heaven. He took a sharp stand against this religious egoism and proclaimed God's love for the whole world. He saw that healing for its own sake was another great danger threatening the true surrender to the will of God, and therefore he eventually gave up healing the sick. In a letter he wrote, "Do not look at yourselves and all your suffering. Look at the suffering of God, whose kingdom has been held up for so long because of the lying spirit of men."

The atmosphere in the household at Bad Boll is described by a guest who visited in 1852, shortly after the father Blumhardt had moved there with his family:

> A spirit of freshness and joy blows through this house, a spirit that gives a vivid impression of what the peace of God is all about, the peace that surpasses all understanding. It pervades everything, practical and spiritual, significant or insignificant. This atmosphere affects the soul as fresh mountain air affects the body.[2]

What a place for children! Here is an anecdote told by this same visitor:

One evening there was a woman at supper with her little four-year-old daughter. She was sitting near Blumhardt, and the child was just behind a pillar. Blumhardt had sent someone to fetch the Bible, as we were waiting for the evening reading to begin. Suddenly, when everything was quiet, Blumhardt's voice was heard: "Peek-a-boo! Peek-a-boo!" And so he had fun with the child for a while. Then he broke off, saying, "So, now be nice and quiet, like a good little girl. We left off at the second half of the second chapter of the Letter to the Ephesians" – which he proceeded to read.[3]

In his biography of Johann Christoph Blumhardt, Friedrich Zündel tells the following story, which also illustrates Blumhardt's great understanding for children and young people:

Now about that difficult age for boys, the "terrible teens" so feared by many educators for its thorns and thistles. Blumhardt found the right way, especially with boys whose hearts were filled with bitterness and confusion, possibly owing to an excessively strict and pious upbringing.

One such boy complained that he had had to put up with too much religious instruction. On the whole he felt quite happy in the free atmosphere of Blumhardt's house, but he was still capable of playing all sorts of tricks. One day a maid came storming into Blumhardt's room: "Pastor Blumhardt, now he went and stole the eggs from the hen house and put this hymnal there instead!" What did Blumhardt do? He said, "The rascal hiding in the boy's heart is also hiding in yours. And behind your anger, aren't you really enjoying it too? We must overcome the boy's mischief in our own hearts. Just put the hymnal back in the hen house. And don't make anything of it."

He told the others also to put things back as they had found them. For a long time the boy was in suspense, waiting, not without a certain impish glee, for the blowup he was sure would follow. When he realized that nobody was going to take any notice, he gave up his nonsense. The hymnal was probably ruined. But to Blumhardt, a boy was worth more.[4]

The father Blumhardt had eight children of his
own. He wanted them to grow up under the influ-
ence of the spirit that ruled in his house. So he
taught his boys at home with the help of a tutor
until they were fifteen or sixteen years old. How
much time and effort that must have cost him!
But he was indeed rewarded when later four of
the five children that lived to grow up and marry
worked with him at Bad Boll or close to him in a
neighboring village. In time he was blessed with
many grandchildren – more than twenty living at
Bad Boll. His son Christoph Friedrich had eleven
children.

Zündel describes how the father, Johann
Christoph Blumhardt, gathered his children and
grandchildren each morning about seven o'clock,
before breakfast, for prayer and singing:

Blumhardt's big family gathered in a large room
for devotions. They were especially for the children, twenty-four of his own grandchildren as
well as other children who had become part of
the family. Here Blumhardt was happy. I think
he looked upon these children as his bodyguard,

his picked troops, and he believed in their pure, simple trust in God and what God wants to bring. He prayed with them as a child among children – not as one stooping to their level, but straight and simple – a fruit of childlike trust.

When the group of parents and children were gathered, Blumhardt would come in, sit down, ring for silence with his little bell, and say a prayer. Then those gathered would sing, "May the Lord bless us," and toward the end of the song all the children would start wriggling.

As soon as the last note died away, all those big enough to walk would start toddling up to Grandfather. The mothers would follow, carrying their babies, and then came the older children. Blumhardt would put his hand on each child, saying, "May the Lord bless you!" and so on down the line.

Of course when there was a special reason, for instance if a child was sick or had a birthday, he would say a few words in addition to this short blessing. The meeting would close with another song. All these songs were sung to tunes that Blumhardt had composed, and the tiniest tot would join in lustily, without being the least disturbance.[5]

It was during these years, when Johann Christoph Blumhardt was a grandfather in his seventies, that most of the excerpts in the first part of this book were written. At this time he published a weekly letter for his many friends, and here he took time to answer questions and write down some of his thoughts on children. In these letters he asks parents, teachers, and adults in general to respect a child's play and innocent joy and not to disturb the child or pester him with grown-up formalities. He even warns us not to offend the angels that accompany a small child. All this he writes with such directness, even bluntness, using down-to-earth Swabian colloquialisms, that it is hard to reproduce his words in English.

Early in his life the father Blumhardt had been moved by the tenderness of Christ. He wrote to his fiancée, Doris Köllner:

This I want to learn, and I need you to help me. It is this gentleness in Jesus that attracted people to him; this is what he called people to. At the same time this gentleness becomes an important tool for the pastor in his handling of sinners. I mean, of course, not just the outer gentleness, but the hidden, inner tenderness that enables us to feel and think in a tender way.[6]

This heart-warming tenderness went out to children and to parents, especially to parents of sick children or to those who had lost a child. He and his wife had also lost two children who lived less than a day and one who died under two years old.

Tenderness and love for children can be strongly felt in the second part of the book, which is made up of extracts from sermons on the subject of children by both father and son Blumhardt.

It is with gratitude for the lives of these two powerful witnesses for the childlike spirit of the kingdom of God that we publish this little book.

ADVICE ON BRINGING UP CHILDREN

Younger Children

From a letter: When my children have been naughty and disobedient, I make it a rule to get them to ask their father's forgiveness. This is very easy for some, and soon they do it quite on their own; but for the others it often costs an inner struggle and considerable strictness before they can be persuaded to do it.

Answer: This rule of yours with your children is quite unfitting and wrong, and you could ruin them with this rigid, moralistic treatment. More often than not, so-called naughtiness and disobedience in children is quite unpremeditated, so that they have no inner feeling of something wrong; they cannot understand what all the fuss is about. Adults so easily call something naughty and disobedient even when this is not the case.

Children are often ordered about too much or in haste; they are hardly able to take in what is expected of them. After all, they are also beings who should be respected. So it is not at all right to make such a big crime out of everything and demand that even the father, who had not been present, should be asked for forgiveness. It is understandable that there is trouble then. But that is by no means all. Many reproaches, then sternness, then scolding, and the children become more and more confused. In the end it leads to great severity and harsh punishment.

Dear mothers, don't do this! This way, all that is childlike and unselfconscious in the children is destroyed, and their endearing ways are taken from them. In regard to anything we ask of little children, it would be a good rule to drop our demands when the children do not respond well because they are not far enough along in their development.[7]

From a letter: My daughter, an adopted child, has been indescribably naughty in the last few

weeks – snitching candy, telling lies, being contrary
and surprisingly rude to grown-ups, more than
ever before. To me the child was not rude but
would give no answer at all when I asked her a
question. She chews her nails, her face twitches,
and her eyes take on a glassy look; and in the end
her whole face sets in a strangely old and hopeless
expression. I believe that even if it cost her her life,
she would not answer at such moments.

Answer: We should be very careful how we treat
this. Severity is the worst thing. Best of all in such
conditions is to do almost nothing until the child
has come to herself, so to speak. This state often
comes about because a child has not been left in
peace – her soul has not been allowed to breathe
freely because someone has been forever occupied with her, especially when several people
are helping. Naughtiness comes from that too.
Never question a child who is in this state you
describe. Even friendliness gets her excited, and
every demand on her makes it worse. So please
stop asking questions straightaway as soon as no
answers come, and do not insist on an answer.

4   In bringing up children, it should be kept very much in mind that it is good to stop and think as soon as any child does not seem to get on well or makes us uneasy. If ever we are driven to prayer, it is in cases such as these. You should turn to God, and I too will think of your child in prayer.[8]

As many people have urged me to say more about bringing up children, I will at last do something about it and write a little more. I did not do so until now because I did not know where to begin; and there is so much I would like to say that I would hardly know where to stop. I was also waiting for questions that would lead to a specific theme, and I would still like to ask for questions. But as none have come, I will write as it comes to me at the moment. There is no lack of opportunity for experience in my house as there are numerous grandchildren growing up all around me.

It is particularly important that the merry, contented, and joyful disposition of one-, two-, and three-year-olds is not disturbed, and in order not to disturb it, those in charge of them must

continually exercise self-denial in the broadest
sense. But just in this area the greatest mistakes
are made. With countless children things soon
go wrong, and then later very wrong, because their
happy disposition in early childhood has not been
treated with consideration and reverence. Instead,
it has been interfered with again and again in all
kinds of seemingly insignificant ways.

Therefore my first request is to refrain from
doing anything that tends to make a child unhappy
and that tears him away from his thoughts, or at
least to consider it carefully; for you could very
easily do differently. A child always thinks for
himself and in his own way. His eyes see all that
is around him, and everything occupies his mind
and urges him to do things with inner joy and
delight, quite innocently. He needs full scope to
let his own thoughts work and to notice things
for himself. That is his first school; he is really
teaching himself. One gets the feeling that angels
are around the children, leading and teaching
them, and whoever is so clumsy as to disturb a
child opposes his angel.

Most of the disturbances a child has to put up with come about because everyone who sees or passes by him quickly has to pick him up and hold him, kiss him, or do something or other with him. One after another may come along and do the same thing. But just at that moment this is not what the child wants, and every child struggles against it, against everyone, even against those he loves most. Then when he struggles, he is held by force and told, "You don't love me." The child becomes more and more unmanageable, instinctively hits out, and begins to cry. Then he is told, "You are so naughty and obstinate!"

Now the complaining begins: the child is self-willed, and the clever advice is given that he must be brought up better and his self-will must be broken, otherwise he will become completely spoiled. So it goes, on and on. The one whose feelings have been hurt gives him a smack, and with holy (or rather unholy) zeal the stick is even resorted to and the poor little mite has to feel it. But who is naughty? Who is self-willed?

The result of it all is that the child is robbed of his sunny disposition, and if it continues, he gradually becomes defiant and unbearable. His own personality has not been respected; others have imposed their personality on his. No wonder many other problems arise in bringing him up![9]

It is important not to disturb the happy disposition of children, especially of small children, because otherwise the natural development of their characters will be ruined. I want to say more about this.

A child, as already mentioned, objects to being picked up by everyone he meets and having to submit unwillingly to all kinds of fondling and caressing. Other people, even if they are near relatives, should leave the child free and not even demand a handshake when the child is busy with something else and does not come of his own accord. Yet often when a child comes into a roomful of people, he is expected to shake hands with each one, perhaps even to say good-day as well, and even to bow or curtsey. "What?" they say to the child, "Don't you know your manners? Go and shake hands," and so on.

We should remember, though, what a burden such demands are on the child. He is expected to be outgoing and concern himself with nothing else, to touch nothing, and turn neither right nor left until he has managed to perform what good manners demand of him, while all the time he longs to do all sorts of other things. Before he knows it, he gets a sharp rebuke, then there is a row, and gone is his happiness. Then maybe on top of it comes the problem of the left hand; what trouble is taken to make him give the proper hand, and how much the child has to listen to, while, in confusion and already a bit bad-tempered, he keeps on offering the left hand.

How quickly we mar our relationship with a child over quite unimportant things, things we should really not bother him with. We just do not put ourselves in the child's shoes and see his needs and innocent wishes. I would like to make an urgent plea once more to all educators always to watch out that the happy nature of a child is protected and that everything that annoys him is done away with. When he is left undisturbed and happy, he learns obedience best of all; then he becomes trusting, and quiet and relaxed, and you can almost see his understanding grow because he is given time to notice things and think about them. When people annoy him and continually correct and criticize him, he becomes rebellious, turns to the bad, and hardens his heart. You can even drive him insane.[10]

A little more on the same subject, and then we can leave it for a while: we often spoil the happy, cheerful nature of children and their childlike contentedness by our habit of making them wait. We always have to get everything done, finish every detail, or at least knit one more row, before satisfying a child's wish or need or pleasing him. When the children become restless because we don't keep our promises and give them the joy of doing what they ask for in all innocence, we call out, "Wait a minute till I've got this finished." The

10 child begs, but one more row must be knitted, a letter must be read or written, and who knows what else has to be done that puts it off longer. We snap at the child, "Wait a bit! Can't you wait a bit?" The child begs all the more persistently and tearfully, until we say, "Can't you leave me in peace? You must learn to wait."

Now the child breaks out crying, sobbing, and wailing. And then: "You naughty child, now you'll certainly not get what you want!" The child is snatched up and taken off. The poor little mite can be heard crying all over the house. This often happens in the nursery. There is an everlasting crying and wailing, and why? Oh, this tiresome procrastination in all the things we owe our children! Between the wails come the impatient words, "You naughty child. You willful child! Wait, you'll get a good smack," and if it gets worse you can hear the stick or the rod or a smack. That really is asking for trouble later.

It is especially important not to make the children wait at table. They simply are not able to wait a long time when they are hungry; and to make them wait can become torture for them. We see this clearly in little children. They get so ravenous that they begin to drool when the mother or the teacher does not hurry. Even older children are often like this, and there is always something unmerciful about making a child wait. Oh, how a child looks forward to something, no matter what, and instead of joy it feels bitter sorrow because of the procrastination of those who have it in their hands to give!

Recently, my dear friend Pastor Wenger from Heinrichsbad visited me. It reminded me of how I was once his father's guest in Bern forty years ago. He was a teacher there and boarded young school children. We had a simple midday meal with them. The father prayed and began to fill the children's plates from the smallest to the oldest. And to me he said, "The children must have their food first because they can't wait." "Oh," I thought at that time already, "that's the right sort of teacher; he puts himself in the children's shoes." Most parents and teachers are in the habit of saying, "Children must wait until the grown-ups are served." I could have kissed Mr. Wenger; his way of doing it warmed my heart right down to my toes.

How much I could still say, but this will be enough for anyone who has open ears.[II]

I wanted to wait a little before writing any more, but in future I will not make any promises about not continuing. I could regret it, and then my friends might take it amiss if I still continue. But I have many small grandchildren around me, and something new keeps on coming to my mind.

Recently I gave our friends this text to learn by heart: "O Lord, help; O Lord, help us to succeed." (Psalm 118:25) It so happened that I gave it also to my little ones to learn. They went back to their room, and a little girl of two-and-a-half learned it especially quickly. The next morning, when the children paid me their morning visit in our living room, I asked the child, "Well, can you say your verse?" She put her head to one side in embarrassment and gave no answer. There was no answer to be got because there were other people around also listening. I let her go.

But it struck me how little children hate to perform on demand. Already when they are asked to come forward, it makes them self-conscious. On their own they will do it with childlike joy and delightful unselfconsciousness, but as soon as it is demanded of them, they are self-conscious, shy, and bashful; they will not or actually cannot do anything, for their will is not behind it.

That applies to everything they have learned, not only to little texts and verses but also to all kinds of tricks such as small children are taught. As soon as they are asked to show what they know or can do, it is all over – they cannot bring it out. If I think about it, there is something precious, yes divine, about this shyness. They cannot be like actors and provide entertainment for grownups and create an empty joy with something serious. Besides, their angels in heaven do not want them to serve the vanity of their parents or come to harm through their own actions.

Yet, dear parents, you do not quite agree, do you? You would be cross if the child did not behave the way you want him to. First you say mildly,

"Well, can't you do it? What? Come on, say it!" Then, "How stupid you are! Go away, I don't like you." Or, "You're being really stubborn now; we must get rid of this obstinacy."

In short, the child is bound to be self-willed, obstinate, and disobedient. And how often does this happen to the poor child! In this way we spoil the joy we have with our children by vain trifles. The child has to pay for the whims of others. How easily something precious in the child is trampled upon! How easily we hurt the little ones, who are in the care of the angels, with our clumsy ways! So leave the children in peace about unnecessary things.

This morning one of my little boys was terribly restless, more than ever before. He kept on looking around and there was no stopping him, but he wasn't naughty. What's the matter with you today? I thought. Suddenly I remembered that his father and mother had gone on a journey the day before; then the child's whole behavior was clear to me.

Take note: everything has a reason with little children! So keep your eyes open! [12]

From a letter: My child has not been well for some weeks and has terrible fits of rage, which we can hardly control.

Answer: What you write about your child has touched my heart, and I sincerely intercede for him. When fits of rage occur, you must on no account take severe measures. Be patient and calm and let him work it off; afterwards, take him to a quiet place, and pray with him and bless him. Keep it short and challenging. Apart from that, be on your guard not to act suddenly in taking something away or restraining him, and never take a thing away or restrain him unnecessarily or at an unsuitable moment. Children do not understand this; they feel unjustly treated, and then something dark comes in. In time things will improve. If you follow this advice, there will be no ill effects in later life. [13]

Whoever adopts children must accept them with all their ingratitude; otherwise it will not go well. To take in children and expect thanks is unnatural and not right. As a rule, it will go badly. Children never show special thanks to those who feed and clothe them, apart from showing love the way children do. They take it quite for granted that we don't let them go hungry or naked, also that we don't do just the minimum for them if they see that we could do a little more. That is theirs by rights, whoever cares for them.

Many who adopt children, however, think that such children should acknowledge and feel awed at the compassion of these people who really owe them nothing – if that is true at all. You simpletons! That is just what they do not feel, so do not demand it of them. Love them without expecting thanks, even if they cause you a lot of trouble; you have to accept them along with their naughtiness. They will feel that, and they will love you for it, but without words.

Often foster children are given what they need,
but without love, and they are made to feel this
even in words. It hurts them deeply and can even
give rise to hate in their hearts. I have known
of two different girls who were prepared to do
anything rather than put up with any more of this
false generosity from their foster parents. Foster
children do not want to have fewer privileges than
the children they live with; they have a sharp eye,
and if they see differences, it hurts them terribly.
Why is that? They are simply children, and they
do not see why one child should have more than
another.

So if you want to adopt children, consider
whether they would really be happier with you
than they would otherwise be, even under miser-
able conditions. And then, if you do adopt them,
do so fully, so that they feel they can really be children with you and make any demand of you and
indulge in their childlike ways without distressing
you. If not, you will receive no thanks either from
them or from our dear Father in heaven.[14]

To a young woman caring for someone else's children:

With all my heart I wish you the Lord's blessing on the task you have been given. I will gladly intercede with our Savior that everything may turn out well for you and the children. By the way, in such a situation it is important not to make too much of the task. Otherwise you will easily make it difficult for yourself and the children and get into unnecessary managing and forcing and anxiety. What more is needed than simply to be with them, love them, play with them, and talk with them, without assuming that you have to do something great or extraordinary? If you do these things I have mentioned, and all the small services attached to them, it will be quite enough. The worst thing for children is being ordered about and corrected. Your task is to serve and to love.[15]

To a young woman: One thing I would advise you that is very important! Small children are hindered most in the proper development of their souls by being hugged and played with too

much, being interrupted in what they want to do,
and passed around from one person to another.
Do not disturb the peace and quiet needed at
this tender age for healthy, sound development.
Remember this![16]

Even the disciples of Jesus became angry when
the children were brought to him. If so many
children come, they thought, little ones and big
ones, unfortunate things may happen. A piece
of furniture may get broken and things may get
dirty. When children are in the living room, things
wear out because children are so active and don't
have much feeling for our knick-knacks and
handsome furniture. They want to handle things
and play: they want to shout and make a rumpus;
they want to be children. That bothers the ladies
and gentlemen, the clever people with culture and
good breeding, people who have laid down rules
of behavior.[17]

On recently tidying up my countless letters, I
suddenly saw yours – unopened! I cannot under-

stand how that came about. I can only think that it must have been mislaid before it was opened.

Your description of the child's illness has touched my heart. How can I resist a childlike plea! I love to pray for children, for we have the word of the Lord asking us to bring them to him. I know many wonderful things that happen especially to children. Certainly, it looks as if some of them are chosen to be among the martyrs of humankind, for many seem to be born only to suffer. That, however, has special significance for God's kingdom. Such children are, as a rule, lovable, obedient, happy, loving Jesus and gladly trusting in him. There is nothing that warms the heart more than seeing such a child.

I do not know how it is with the dear little girl you tell about, who loves Jesus so much. Perhaps she may improve or even recover. But it seems to me that her sickness has already taken deep root. Meanwhile we will keep turning to our Lord. He will surely answer our prayer in some way, if only that the child feels his loving presence. I would advise you especially not to let all the possibilities

of medical skill be exhausted on the poor child.
I hesitate to say much about this; but it is certain
that the simplest treatment is always the best in
such cases of unexplained sickness.

Greet the dear child and her parents, too, from
me and tell her that a faraway friend is praying
for her and that through his prayer many children
have been helped. He asks her to be patient and
to go on loving Jesus even if she has to suffer for
some time, and he sends her these two little verses
for a keepsake.[18]

Comfort for a mother whose child has died:

Of this much I am certain, that a child such as
this one who was called to eternity could not be
held back. Even as I was beginning to pray for
him, I had a slight feeling that you would have to
sacrifice this child.

Usually children whose spirits reach upwards
so clearly are not for this world. Parents should
consider it a blessing that these children are with
our Savior, for I am convinced they can serve
as angels. They are fighting souls with a task in

eternity. Who can tell how far-reaching this is, and
what a help it might be to their families?

Let that be enough. Never say that our Lord
should rather have taken this or that child. The
Lord did not simply want any child from you – he
wanted that particular child. For the others, as for
all of us, there remains the fight here on earth,
certainly a different and much harder fight.[19]

Jesus is still in Capernaum, in the intimate circle
of his disciples, telling them more about what they
should take to heart. The child he had placed in
their midst may still have been there, because he
talks about *these* children: "See that you do not
despise one of these little ones; for I tell you that in
heaven their angels always behold the face of my
Father who is in heaven." (Matt. 18:10)

To our Lord, despising the little ones means
not being eager and willing to lead them to Jesus
and ensure that they are his. It is easy for us to
look down on the little ones – and the young
people – and not be willing to pull ourselves
together and help them and further them in their

faith. Some people act as though it were not
worthwhile to concern themselves with the little
ones in spiritual matters, thinking they will not
remember or understand or appreciate it. It is part
of despising the little ones if we trust too little in
their understanding and their sensitivity in matters
of the spirit. Yet we could easily observe that
the opposite is true. Children, especially in their
personal relationship with Jesus, are even more
receptive, yes, more understanding than adults.
For many adults are used to listening superficially,
while little ones do not miss the smallest or most
insignificant thing.

It is clear that we have to come down a bit
from the high horse of reason on which we enjoy
sitting. We have to be simple and take time to
think how to make things understandable to the
little ones. We have to become children again, and
some find that too hard. How much we have to
learn to deny ourselves for the little ones! Yet there
is nothing more rewarding than making an effort
for children; they are often remarkably open to
higher things, if we only knew how to reach them.

Of course, what we do for children and what they gain from it remains mostly unnoticed; and many people are only interested in making an impression in the world with whatever they do.

Our Lord tells us something that should encourage us to give ourselves as much as possible for the little ones. He says, "Their angels always behold the face of my Father who is in heaven." Our heavenly Father always gives these angels to the children to watch over them. The children are not left alone, not abandoned, even when people do not take much notice of them. Children have something individually precious in the eyes of God. But apart from that, the more the parents and relatives commend their children to God's care, the more certain and far-reaching is the protection granted by our Father in heaven. If parents were more constant and faithful in this, they could prevent many things that happen to their little ones simply because they do not commend them often enough to God's protection or give them enough personal care.

When the Savior speaks of "their angels in heaven," we should not think of the special guardian angel given to each child. We tend to elaborate the idea of guardian angels almost to the point of idolatry, as though angels were the children's gods. Yet the angels only carry out God's will; they are not allowed to do the least thing on their own. Therefore, when we think of the angels of our Father, we must think of the heavenly Father himself, and we would do well to think of our Lord more than of the angels. Yet the thought of angels does help us to believe in the heavenly care and protection given to us and our children.

Our text says that the angels sent to protect the little ones "always behold the face of my Father who is in heaven." That means that they are constantly giving an account to our Father about those in their care: how they are, how they are treated, who is good to them and takes care of them; who disdains and despises them, does not care about them, or even provokes and ill-treats them. Our Father in heaven will at least take note,

if we may say so, of all these things. So we can see
that he looks on us according to the way we treat
children.[20]

The angels come straightaway to anyone who
seeks Jesus the crucified and really means it, like
the women on Easter morning. To them, the
atmosphere of angels became quite natural, and
everything that took place then was as though it
had to be just that way. That is the best, when the
angels above are a natural part of our lives. Children
often have this feeling, but older people do not, or
very seldom.[21]

Older Children

Someone asked me in a letter why it so often happens that the respect due to parents is not forthcoming from adolescent and grown-up children, and whether the fault is in the parents or the children.

When I am asked such questions, I can only talk to those who ask me, not to those about whom the question is raised; so those who have the question must put up with it if I talk mostly about their mistakes and failings. And so I am pointing out to my questioner several of the mistakes that are often made. But the young nosey parkers need not hear about that. However, they should realize how hard it is to keep together with them on the right track.

Many parents demand too much submission from their adolescent or adult children; they put a certain pressure on them even in trifling matters, as if they were still small children. They are intolerant toward them and do not respect enough the special wishes they might have; even small daily wishes are not respected. Parents correct, punish, and find fault far too much, censure too strongly for accidents and carelessness, so that there is never a friendly conversation and never an atmosphere of friendliness; strictness and disapproval is all the young people feel from their parents.

Such parents are constantly after their children and give them no independence. They do not show them enough trust and continually accuse them of lack of love, respect, and obedience. So the children have no joy in life, and it even happens that their greatest longing is to get away from home because their own personality is unfulfilled. They become depressed and sulky, sad, melancholy, obstinate, and contrary, and then there are scenes that wreck everything. And so they seem to lose the respect they owe their parents.

Now I have written so much about this subject
because in writing I am thinking of many people,
not just the one who asked the question. But perhaps a little of what I wrote can be of help to her.

Children, in short, must *honor* and *respect* their
parents; but parents also should gradually learn to
honor and respect their children.

But take note, you children – I have not been
speaking to you. You don't need to hear and see
any of this. If you ask me, I know what I will tell
you.[22]

You complain that when your children were
little it was so easy to tell them about Jesus and
lead them to him, but now that they are growing
up you do not find the way to their hearts. Even
reading the Bible together is difficult, let alone
talking about what has been read.

All this is quite natural. Grown-up children
need more than little children, and mothers do
not always know how to go beyond the help they
gave their little ones and meet the spiritual needs
of grown-up children. So everything is familiar

and boring to the latter because the words do not speak to their age range and nothing is offered to help them go deeper.

Because of this it is better simply to keep a Christian atmosphere among them than to use many words. Rather give up reading the Bible together, apart from what is part of the daily routine of the home, because for older children it becomes an unpleasant compulsion that destroys more than it helps. Altogether, mothers must stop treating older children as the objects of continual preaching. They should begin to treat them as people who can preach to themselves, and such trust will be most likely to win them. If not, then something is missing.[23]

From a letter: In your leaflet of April 8, 1876, there is an article about the relationship between parents and their grown-up children. May I ask you to say something now for the instruction of us children?

Answer: It is nice that you ask, because I would not have liked to say anything without being asked.

Actually I do not have much more to say than what
you can find out for yourselves from the article;
you can read everything between the lines. Pick up
the article, and let me go through it with you.

First and foremost, you must remember that
it is never in any circumstances right to refuse
your parents the respect due to them, least of all
because you believe they are not treating you right.
They should never get the feeling that your respect
for them is dwindling.

When parents find it difficult to keep on the
right track with their grown-up children, it is just
because the children are so quick to think they
have a right to complain and let their parents
feel that they are dissatisfied, and therefore they
behave in an improper way. When parents have
to be quiet in front of grumbling children, things
are not going in the right direction in God's eyes.
If parents demand submission, be submissive, and
if you do that gladly, your parents will be more
lenient toward you. If you feel you have too little
say, there is perhaps a reason for it – perhaps you
put your word in too often. If your wishes are

not granted often enough, you probably have too many; and sometimes you also pursue your wishes on your own more than you should. Sometimes children have also something high and mighty about them, and in their parents' house that won't do. Parents are after all master in their own house.

Further, be more courteous and more punctual so that you do not need to be corrected or punished or admonished so often. Rather, learn to do everything properly and promptly and accurately.

When children grow older, they often do not want to learn anything anymore or be told anything, because they think they know it all; yet how good this would be for them. In particular they feel far above the housemaids and domestics. A modest, undemanding attitude to servants is the nicest one that can be found in children. When servants sigh and groan about children, or still worse, give notice because of them, that is really bad.

We would often like to give you your independence, if you could bear it. You want more trust

shown you – then you must let it be tested beforehand. Aren't you sometimes a bit too dreamy
and moody, so that you do not respond when
your parents complain about you? You ought to
improve in that. Altogether, it should never happen
that you are peevish, obstinate, headstrong, or
contrary toward your parents. And when there
are scenes, I am inclined to think that the fault
lies mostly with the children. Where is your self-
denial, compassion, modesty, and humility?

Some children can hardly be torn away from
reading novels, and when they do leave their books,
they set about their work with grumbling and with
a bad grace. When children complain a lot that
they don't count enough, how is it if their parents
don't count?

But forgive me, dear children, especially you
who are asking the questions. Quite without noticing it, I started to talk about rude and naughty
children. But wait a minute! Are you not all at
times a bit rude and naughty? Do not forget your
Savior, who wants so very much to love you! Do
not forget his words and ways. If he loves you, so

will your parents, and you will love them! May he remain yours all your life long. Savior, be thou our help![24]

How can we help the Savior on earth to build up God's kingdom? Where is the Savior? The only answer I know to this question is: In your heart! If he is not in your heart, he is nowhere.

It is an illusion to think you are bringing a child to the Savior by rushing him to church and having him baptized, if afterwards you bring him up in your filth at home. Millions of children are baptized and then grow up into the human or fleshly ways of their parents instead of in the ways of Jesus. Or if you think your children will come to Jesus by being taught Bible texts and having Bible lessons in school, you are wrong again.

You cannot bring your children to Christ if you have him only in your Bible or in your private rituals and not in your heart. "Let the children come to *me*" –not to your pious customs, your Christian traditions, but "to *me*." We keep trying to achieve things by means of rules. Because the

Spirit is missing, we try to do things mechanically.
But it does not work, and then there is the usual
complaint about how bad young people are. While
children are small, we keep them under our thumb
and force them to accept all kinds of ideas. But as
they grow up they go their own way regardless.
You can never keep a hold on your child, but the
Savior can keep a hold on him. You cannot force
anything by your intellect; the only way you can
accomplish anything is by living in repentance and
brokenness about yourself, so that the Savior can
grow to be something in you. All children, big and
little, want to come to Jesus; if you try to drag
your child into the kingdom of heaven by means
of outward piety, he will run out of your pious
house faster than children from other homes,
where they are likely to stay and be decent and
well-behaved.

The only way, then, is to use the sword against
your own hearts. Don't accuse your children
when they go wrong – accuse yourselves! Be hard
on yourselves; wield the sword against your own
hearts, for it is our fault when our children do not

turn out well. The "old Adam" in us has to give
way and no longer have a say. Christ alone must
count, and then our children will have something
firm to hold on to. Then it will make no difference
what the schools are like or what the churches
are like. If we know the children are in his hands,
not ours, we can cheerfully let them go. Any child
in any city, if he is in the Savior's hands, is more
protected than he would be in his own home if
the Savior is not allowed in there. God is stronger
than the whole world, and Jesus is victor. He holds
everyone and everything firmly in his hands. But
we older ones, too, have to become children and
not want to be anything great. For even if we were
so religious that the whole world talked about us,
we still wouldn't get into God's kingdom unless
we became children. We have to be children, that
is simply a fact; it is the unshakable law of the
kingdom of heaven.[25]

The goal of education is always to produce
masterminds. That, so to speak, is the cloven hoof
in our education. Masterminds are constantly

being produced. Anyone who goes to college
thinks he can dominate others who have not had a
college education. If someone is put into office, he
thinks he can dominate others because of his posi-
tion. This runs through everything. A man even
gets the idea that simply because he has money
and property and worldly advantages, he can
dominate others.[26]

We need to know how to obey God in our time.
That is basic, and I thank my father for teaching
us that from childhood on. Let me boast a little
and tell you that as far as the kingdom of God was
concerned, my father was outstanding in all of
Europe. His passing, like his life, was little noticed;
the pious theologians looked down on him. But
wait a bit, and you will see him shine from heaven.
He knew how to obey, and he helped those who
held faith with him to become free and find an intimate understanding of God's work in the world.
And so we feel quite at home in all that God does
and is and wants in our time.

But in order to find that understanding, we need to be taught wisely. We as children were taught like this; not about the church, the congregation, or the community, *but only and exclusively about the kingdom of God.* Already when I was only three or four years old, my father used to call us into his study and show us his big maps, and say, "You must conquer the world; God's kingdom has to come into the whole world." He saw beyond the parsonage, beyond Möttlingen and Bad Boll – out into the world.[27]

The Twelve-year-old Jesus in the Temple

This Sunday I want to address the children in a special way, using Luke 2:41–52. So it is delightful that we have a story of Jesus as a child. The child Jesus comes into our midst today with his completely childlike nature and speaks to us as to children. He had already learned a great deal in his twelve years.

In Israel there was the good custom of going to Jerusalem each year for the festival. Mothers even took their tiny babies along. That was a long, long journey, on camels, or donkeys, or on foot. People had to spend nights out in the open, and it always took four or five days to travel from Nazareth to Jerusalem. So you can imagine how much the children looked forward to that. Just to travel with so many people who all were on their way to Jerusalem was a great festival in itself. They all journeyed with a holy purpose. The memory of what God had done for the people of Israel lived in them. And this memory was revived in the temple at Jerusalem. For days beforehand, families would talk together about the temple, about the sacrifice, and about the history of Israel from Abraham on. And that was what they lived in: God among his people.

So it was that the twelve-year-old Jesus also went to the temple with his parents, surely with great joy.

He came into the great tumult of the festival. It is estimated that about one million people came there for the festival from all over the place – from Galilee, Samaria, and Judea. There they gathered and rejoiced in their God, remembering the history of Israel, in which God had revealed himself so wonderfully. And in the bustle of the festival, the boy – Jesus – got lost. He was like a lost

lamb. So already as a child he felt what it meant
not to know where to look for help.

The older people were very busy. Naturally in
a city like that, with so many sights to see and so
many opportunities to buy things, one little boy
is easily forgotten. There was no one to concern
himself with the boy, and before his parents realized it, they had lost sight of him. Their fellow
travelers were not aware of him either. And all
at once the boy noticed that he was lost. In that
milling crowd of people in Jerusalem with its
narrow streets, its big shops and markets, he was
completely alone. What was he to do now?

Deep down he recalled that he was a child
of God; and a child of God cannot get lost. As
he wandered through the streets, unable to find
his parents, he must have thought, "Where do I
belong?" And then it dawned on him: I belong to
God! He quickly found the place where people
went to speak about his Father in heaven. And he
went into the temple.

There were always certain men in the temple
who taught the people. And that is where this

twelve-year-old boy went, timidly perhaps, until he came to where the teachers were sitting, ready to give instruction to anyone who came. Soon the boy was good friends with the old scribes and rabbis. At first they looked at him in surprise, for they seldom met a boy of his age who had such a thirst for knowledge about God. But Jesus was coming into "his Father's business."

At first his parents did not worry, and continued on their homeward journey. At the first stopping place they looked and looked; but the boy was nowhere to be found. It is about a four-hour journey from Jerusalem to that first stopping place. It has a gushing spring, and the land is fertile.

Here his parents turned around to go back, and now they were looking for the boy with a great deal of anxiety. His mother naturally felt a great responsibility for this firstborn son of hers. She still remembered all those words that she had heard at the time of his birth. And most likely we have Mary to thank for the fact that we still have this wonderful story today. Luke, who tells us this story, says expressly that he inquired everywhere

for stories about Jesus; he is certain to have gone
to see the mother of Jesus and heard from her the
stories we love so much. So we should be very
grateful to Mary; she kept it all in her heart.

And now her faithful heart heard another
special word when she found her son in the temple
at last. She heard him say the words that went
out into all the world like a trumpet blast and still
move our hearts today: "Do you not know that
I must be about my Father's business? Has it not
been said from my birth on that I belong to him
who made heaven and earth and holds them in his
hand? This is where I have to be: in the dwelling
place of this great God, my Father."

So the twelve-year-old boy becomes a teacher
among us. He teaches you children, and he teaches
all of us. When we feel lonely, when we are
forlorn, we know where to go. Wherever there is
a real interest in God and in what he has done and
still wants to do, there is our Father's house, God's
house. That will never come to an end; and if we
seek Jesus, we will know where to go. We will find
the Lord Jesus where the Father of all men has

built himself a house, a house with living hearts that care about him. Never, never will God forsake the earth. Somehow, somewhere, we can always find our Father's house.

So my dear children, this is what we want the Savior to teach us. Keep his words in your hearts! Keep God's deeds in your hearts! Believe like children! You can feel just like the twelve-year-old Jesus. Whenever things are hard for you on earth, remember in your heart: "I belong where my Father's house is."[28]

The Savior and Children

Some people came to him bringing little children for him to touch. The disciples scolded them. When Jesus saw this, he was indignant and told them, "Let the children come to me; do not hinder them; for the kingdom of God belongs to such as these. Truly, I tell you, whoever does not accept the kingdom of God like a little child will never enter it." And he took them in his arms and blessed them, laying his hands upon them. (Mark 10:13–16)

Today we are reminded of Jesus' attitude to little children, how he looked at them and felt drawn to them. We might say that just because he was once a child himself, he had a special feeling for children; and because he remained a child and kept his childlike spirit, he had the deepest love, tenderness, and affection for them. It is a fact even nowadays that a person who has stopped being a child himself cannot stand children; he sends them away and has no use for them. But if even a trace of childlikeness is left in a man's heart, he feels attracted to children, he caresses and hugs them – in a word, he is happy in their company.

Now we have heard this story that is told about Jesus as the friend of little children. He always had serious things to talk about and to do; he was occupied with the needy, the unhappy, the sick, and the poor, and to all of them he was a genuine friend and wonderful Savior. Babies, too, are needy in their dependence on other people; they cannot speak for themselves or do anything for themselves. Children are helpless creatures – the smaller, the more helpless. So we can take it for granted that Jesus would not have had a distant manner with them or have said, as some do, "I can't speak to these children, they are much too young! They should go to their nursemaids. What is the use of taking time for them? I need adults who can

understand me and whose hearts I can reach." He
could never have thought like that.

Mark tells us here that people brought little
children to him. These must have been mothers
who wanted the best for their children; who
were happy only when their children were happy,
mothers who had already experienced the Savior
and had been moved by him, who must have felt
in their hearts something of the blessing and well-
being that came from the words they heard him
speak. Their hearts must have been filled with
happiness, and so when these mothers looked at
their little ones, they thought, "Why should they
be less fortunate than I? Should they be thought
less of than I? If only they were as fortunate as I
am! If only they had received the blessing I have
and had a Savior like mine!" These mothers were
not happy at the thought that their children should
be less close to Jesus than they themselves, or less
important in his eyes. There is a natural longing,
laid by God in every mother's heart, to bring children to Jesus so that the little ones may receive
from him the same blessing their mothers received.

And now? What was to be done with such little ones? Of course Jesus could not talk to them; they would not have understood him. He could not speak words of encouragement to them; there was nothing he could do with them. But their mothers knew very well what the Savior could do: he could touch them! The one thing we can do with little children is to lead them by the hand, caress them, bless them, or take them in our arms and rock them gently – that is all we can do.

The mothers had seen with their own eyes how when he touched the sick, they were healed; when he touched the eyes of the blind, they received sight; when he laid his fingers on the tip of a dumb man's tongue, the man was able to speak; when he placed his fingers in the ears of a deaf man, the man was able to hear. They may have heard of the woman who said to herself, "If only I could touch the hem of his garment, I would get well." She did and was healed. No wonder the mothers thought it would not be in vain if the Lord Jesus were to lay his hands on their children. It would go right through their whole bodies, and a wonderful

power from God would come upon them to
awaken something in their hearts to lay in them a
seed of divine strength and of God's spirit in Jesus.
And this seed would protect each of these little
ones and would keep him safe in the midst of this
world's temptations, right to the end of his life.

Was it right of these mothers to think as they
did? Why, of course it was! They were quite right!
I would be glad if the Savior had touched my children. I am sure that a child upon whom the Savior's
hand once lay could never be lost, for a divine seed
remains in that child. I am sure the Lord would
have marked that child to be his own forever.

Maybe the parents of some of those children
were worried about them because they were sick
or naughty. We know how often children are ill,
how sickly some of them are as they grow up, how
much they cry, how many hidden ailments and
pains they have to suffer. They cry a lot and cannot
say what is wrong, and the parents cannot find
out either. In many a home there is great sorrow.
Nothing is more painful than to hear a child crying
day and night and not know how to help him.

Among those brought to Jesus there may have
been children who suffered terribly, perhaps from
some obvious ailment. Their parents figured that
if adults could recover their health, couldn't the
same happen to these poor little mites? They are
driven to say, "Have pity on them; if thou canst do
anything, help our dear children." Surely it will not
have been in vain that he touched them.

How well and happy those children must have
felt as the Lord Jesus laid his hands on them, and
how delighted and joyful their mothers must have
been as they took them home, knowing that from
then on they need not worry so much about their
children but could rejoice in them.

But there are other children, children who are
obstinate, quarrelsome, irritable, disagreeable,
naughty, disobedient, angry, or malicious from an
early age on. That, too, is terrible for their parents.
And it can happen that no punishment helps,
that is, if they are old enough to be punished; on
the contrary, it gets worse and worse. The more
they are punished, the more obstinate, sulky, and

resistant they become. That kind of thing happens many times. Often the cause is a lack of wisdom and understanding on the part of parents. They fuss over their children, irritate them in all kinds of ways, expect more of them than their tender nature can respond to, demand too much, are too quick and too severe with the stick, and are apt to come down hard on a child for things of which he is as innocent as a lamb. Parents who are impatient with their children will slap them whatever they do. Then the children start to cry and end up by becoming unbearable, or should we say, cross and unhappy. In this unhappy atmosphere, these children are being thoughtlessly pulled to pieces and harmed to the point of not knowing anymore where they are. They become deeply unhappy because of the heartlessness of adults. Parents are not even the worst. Teachers and nursemaids often go much too far; they plague and harass the children, particularly when they are alone with them, and the result is a child as young as two or three who looks as though he is going to turn into a little demon.

Then some people are so unwise as to force children to pray. The child has to listen to words repeated to him for fifteen minutes, for half an hour, and he gets bored. But woe to him if he says, "I don't want to pray." He does not mean to be irreverent; he simply cannot do it; he can't stand it. Still, some parents drive their children almost to distraction with praying. Such things make for behavior that is twisted, violent, and disobedient, and this in turn makes these poor, foolish parents suffer. In those cases there is need for great wisdom and enlightenment, and that has often been the help.

There are times, too, when a child is as though possessed by an evil spirit or at least as though an evil spirit were working in him and making him stubborn and resistant. He cannot help being furious; he cannot help being disobedient, insufferable, and quarrelsome. He screams and throws a tantrum. When a child is in such a state that he holds his breath and you think he is going to suffocate, he cannot help it. It is not hard to see that something is wrong with this child, and the worst we can do is to use the stick. When this happens, we have to be gentle and submit to the Lord, raise our eyes to him and plead, "Lord, have mercy and help thou!"

You see, children like these were probably also brought to the Savior. Then the devil had to back out, the powers of darkness had to yield; the children felt good and became free, and all of a sudden they were quite different; all of a sudden their troubles had vanished. Surely that is what many mothers experienced with their little ones when they brought them to the Savior. It was this kind of concern that drove them to bring him their children, and it surely was not in vain. From that moment on the divine power of God's blessing will have worked in the children, instead of the dark powers. All these things the mothers expected from a touch of the Savior's hands upon their little ones.

But now the question is, how will they get to the Lord? For he was always surrounded by people; there was always a crowd around him. Weeping adults, not just weeping children but people in all kinds of trouble, pressed around him, people whose hearts were heavy. And on top of that the mothers came along with their screaming children! Oh, you dear mothers! The disciples saw them coming and scolded them: "What are you doing here with your children? Why don't you keep them at home! Who has time for your children? Look at all these people pushing, and now you come and bother the Lord!" – however they may have said it, politely or rudely, they simply told them to go away. Now we all know that there are heartless people, people who have no feeling for a child when they see him. So let us not think too harshly of the disciples. But they must have been unkind, else it would not be said that the Lord was indignant. And we want to take it to heart and be very careful not to treat little children, who in a special way belong to the Lord Jesus, in a cold, unfeeling way or look down on them. Besides, there is nothing more hurting for a mother than to feel that her child is despised; that pierces her heart like a knife. The little ones do not feel it quite like their parents; but the parents feel deeply hurt. Nothing is more crushing for a mother's heart than to know that her children are despised, abused, or pushed aside. A mother has no greater treasure on earth than her children; she would give up all she has, her home, money, fields, everything, for the sake of her children. She would leap into the fire a hundred times to snatch her child from the flames. That is why it hurts her so much to be insulted on account of her child.

The Lord also felt the pain in his heart; in this case he felt it more keenly than the mothers, who were in a sense used to seeing children treated that way. But the Lord Jesus felt the hurt, and we will be held accountable for the pain we cause him even now, over and over again, by being cold and hardhearted toward children. Many a man thinks at the end of his life of all his sins – all, that is, except those committed against children. If we have treated any child, especially an older child, in a way that was not fatherly or motherly but tyrannical and even devilish, it is important to remember that such things are not so quickly blotted out in the book of our sins.

At times I am in a quandary when, in talks or letters, I hear of people whose consciences are struck because they have sinned against children in such a way that the sting of sin was awakened in those children. A man may be deeply remorseful and have a longing to repent yet be unable to find peace, because he feels he taught a child something that might cause the child's damnation: he misled him, corrupted him, and introduced him to sin. It is a struggle for the man's conscience to find peace, and I myself often find it hard to know how to comfort him. I am convinced, however, and have experienced, that our merciful Savior does miracles in people in that kind of need if they truly repent. I did not want to ignore this aspect, since we are talking about children today.

We adults may well say, "Oh, that we could become children again!" For no one who is not a child can enter the kingdom of heaven. "Whoever does not accept the kingdom of God like a little child will never enter it" (Mark 10:15). Try as we

may to become children again, we seem to be
incapable of it; we are too far from it. And who
is farthest from being a child? The independent
person.

When a child no longer needs father or mother,
he has stopped being a child. When a child has
no need of a friend, a helper, a guardian, he is
no longer a child. In other words, when we no
longer listen to anyone, no longer accept anything,
are no longer able to make friends with another,
when we have no need of a Savior and think we
can walk into heaven on our own two feet, when
we become independent and no longer want to
obey anyone, when we have lost our flexibility,
our submission to older people, our modesty, our
warmth of heart–then we are children no longer.
A child is one who needs his parents; whoever does
not want father or mother anymore is not a child.
We should at all times have the attitude of needing
a father and a mother.

And now to close: "And he took them in his
arms and blessed them, laying his hands upon
them" (Mark 10:16). What a great moment! Powers

58   from on high, powers from God, overflowed and
     streamed down upon these children.

     May all of us and each one we meet, espe-
     cially children, be given the Spirit and power from
     above, so that we may have eternal life! Amen.[29]

Let the Children Come to Me

Thoughts on Mark 10:13–16

Dear friends, if your heart longs for God's kingdom, the sight of a little child will do you good. It will do you good for God's sake, that is. Not because a child is such a cute little thing, as people say, or something nice to play with, to entertain you, but because he is something God can use, something precious to God, a jewel on earth.[30]

This Sunday [January 9, 1910] is called Children's Sunday. It should mean something to the children and bring them close to our hearts, and make us glad and thankful that we, too, can be little children. It places the children in God's kingdom, even the smallest ones, whom we hardly consider at all and treat almost like playthings. We hug them and kiss them but still think they have nothing to say. Yet in God's kingdom it is quite different; the kingdom blossoms again and again in little children. When we have many, many children around us, we can say, "This is the kingdom of God." It is from them that the Father in heaven creates the strength he needs on earth to reach men's hearts, which are smothered under the rubble of their earthly existence to a point where the child in them is no longer visible. Our Father in heaven needs children. And you children who are here again today and are back at school, remember that you belong to the kingdom of God. Just exactly the part of you that is still completely childlike, that has not yet been educated and formed, that came straight from the hand of God – that is the part that belongs to the kingdom of God. Thinking of the Savior when he says, "Let the children come to me, do not hinder them; for to such belongs the kingdom of God," I want to tell all you children to remember that Jesus gave

you the first right to enter the kingdom of heaven
or to feel that you are in the kingdom.

We can sense the kingdom of heaven; a childlike heart can feel it, for it is all around us. In
every sunbeam that shines on us, in every little
wild flower, in everything that lives and moves on
earth, there is something of the kingdom of God.
There is something of beauty that can touch our
hearts and teach us in a way that we can hardly
learn from men's words. There is something real
of the kingdom of heaven already on our earth,
and our task is to learn to see this. And the children, though they often do not know where their
happiness comes from again and again – their
new courage, new confidence, and new joy – they
can always think, "This comes to me from the
kingdom of heaven." The kingdom of heaven
is all around us. And each time we have to look
into the world of men and have to go into it, we
should bring with us the kingdom of heaven that
surrounds us and affects us so much. Everything
that comes to us from this heavenly kingdom

speaks to us for the good, to give comfort and make us joyful.[31]

What Jesus is saying is: "Why don't you let the little children come to me? What sort of image have you made of man? Who created man? Look at a little child – is he not holy? Look at the heart and mind of a child. Do they not come from God? Let the children come to me – they are the way God made them. Let them come; this is where God wants to begin his new kingdom."

Jesus is among his people: he sees the little children, and he also sees the child in the older, grown-up people. There still is a child in each of us. If you let a child be a child, he is happy. If a person can be like a child again, he is happy. A child is subject to his father, not to any other person. If we want to let people be children, if we do what Jesus says we should, then we have to think of them as being under the Father and nobody else. A preacher can let the children gather around him if he likes, but he must not take the place of the Father; he must know that they are under God. The disciples of Jesus are not allowed to rule; they must never command, otherwise they would destroy these little ones. It is an offense to the child in children if anyone but God rules. That is the way the kingdom of God is formed.[32]

If we love the kingdom of God and seek it on earth, and wonder where we can find something that will serve God for his kingdom, then seeing a little child makes us think, "Yes, there is something that God can use!" Even if the child is sick or gives us trouble, this does not put us off if we think of God and his kingdom, for even in his pain a child serves God. Woe to anyone who gets angry because a child cries in pain. He has forgotten God and forgotten that the kingdom of heaven belongs to the children.

We can serve God by noticing children, protecting them, and caring for them for his sake. We can serve God by bearing them on our hearts, asking our Father in heaven to send his angels to protect these precious pieces of gold that can still serve him in this evil world, to keep them for his kingdom and not let them be lost. Whenever we see a child, we should look into ourselves in search of the child within us adults that maybe still lingers there. We can bring out this child in us again and strip off all that has covered him up so he can come before God's countenance again – this poor crippled child that could not be used for God's kingdom in his sinfulness and deformity and godlessness because he had so much that was human mixed up in him.[33]

It is refreshing for Jesus when people who are healthy and normal and are not driven by a particular outward need come to him to help in God's kingdom. These are the mothers! A mother, a real mother with a little child, thinks day and night about the welfare of the little one in her arms. A mother knows what dangers the child will have to encounter as he grows up. She does not let the father reassure her when he makes light of things and says that the children have to find their own way.

A mother worries, for she carries the burden, and she often sees much deeper than the father just where the child is in danger. Apart from this she has the outward care too. A small child is often sick, and it is the mother who has to sit at the bedside in tears and nurse him. A mother feels the child's pain, and every cry is like a sword piercing her heart, but she has to bear it. Her husband can go off to work and say, "I can't stand all this crying." But the mother has to stay – there she sits!

The burden she carries is a divine one, for it is God who gave her the child; and this often works in a mother's heart in such a way that she finds the right way with children faster than other people, faster than the father or brothers and sisters or the teachers. A mother turns to God with her child sooner than others do. Others, as for instance in schools or institutions, reach for a stick or use detention. But a mother is much more likely to think: This child needs God's help.

It is as if this God-given burden quietly teaches the motherly heart to do a true service to God.

So when these mothers bring their little children, the Savior's heart leaps for joy. In this world that gives him so much trouble, that is like a refreshing drink to him. For little children seem like people who can be used in the kingdom of heaven just as they are. A dear little child could be taken straight to heaven. And yet we want them to live. It almost seems a pity; it makes you wish that God's kingdom would come soon so that the little children could go right in and wouldn't have to turn into misshapen old people.[34]

In the world of men there are many depressing things that people have contrived for themselves and that affect their thoughts. They have even allowed these things to enter their hearts and become the source of all kinds of evil that puts a heavy burden on children whom God created. Then many children, even very small children, have to suffer. It is not easy to grow up in this world.

When a little child comes into the world and is allowed to grow for a time, it is as though we are surrounded by the pure air of heaven; we feel

that something is really born of God. I feel it is a
witness to our Father in heaven that our children,
even those born of quite sinful parents, look at us
so gaily, in such a pure and happy way; when their
eyes meet ours, we feel as if an angel from heaven
were looking at us – oh, so pure, so holy, and so
joyful, even in the poorest circumstances, even
where all kinds of evil rule. When such a little
child looks at us, it is like a light in the darkness.

But there is also a struggle going on in such a
child, and it moves us when we see him suffering
and looking at us pleadingly with innocent eyes as
if to say, "Can't you help me?" Many a mother's
heart has nearly been broken to see the pleading
eyes of her little child and not be able to help him.
This happens right in front of our eyes. There is a
fight against the evil of the world, and nowhere is
this fight seen more clearly than in children.[35]

The Savior loves to have children brought to
him. Even though he sees in them disease and
the roots of various evils, still, if they were taken
into heaven just as they are, they would not give

the angels much trouble and would soon be fit for
heaven and an encouraging sight for the Savior.[36]

What then should we wish for our children?
What should we wish for them and do for them as
we see them grow up, whether ailing or healthy,
when we have to introduce them to the difficulties
of life, when we have to accustom them early to
hard work? How can we help them when we have
to see them going into the harsh, coarse, rude
atmosphere that meets them on the streets and
everywhere? My dear friends, if we want to be of
any help, we must become children ourselves and
meet our children as children, and remember that
these little ones belong to Jesus.[37]

1. A. Albers, "Von Spengler zu Blumhardt," *Das neue Werk; Der Christ im Volksstaat,* 1920/1921, p. 405.

2. Friedrich Zuendel, *Pfarrer Johann Christoph Blumhardt, ein Lebensbild* (Zürich, 1881), p. 451.

3. *Ibid.,* pp. 451–452.

4. *Ibid.,* pp. 364–365.

5. *Ibid.,* p. 445.

6. *Ibid.,* p. 51.

7. Johann Christoph Blumhardt, *Blätter aus Bad Boll für seine Freunde* (Stuttgart, 1874), p. 344.

8. *Ibid.,* p. 352.

9. Johann Christoph Blumhardt, *Blätter aus Bad Boll* (1875), p. 32.

10. *Ibid.,* p. 40.

11. *Ibid.,* p. 48.

12. *Ibid.,* p. 56.

13. Johann Christoph Blumhardt, *Blätter aus Bad Boll* (1873), p. 72.

14. *Ibid.,* p. 32.

15. Friedrich Zuendel, *Pfarrer Johann Christoph Blumhardt, ein Lebensbild* (Zürich, 1881), p. 364.

16. *Ibid.,* p. 364.

17. Christoph Friedrich Blumhardt, *Ihr Menschen seid Gottes! Predigten und Andachten aus den Jahren 1896 bis 1900,* ed. R. Lejeune (Zürich & Leipzig, 1936), p. 429.

18. Friedrich Zuendel, *Pfarrer Johann Christoph Blumhardt, ein Lebensbild* (Zürich, 1881), p. 480.

19. Johann Christoph Blumhardt, *Blätter aus Bad Boll* (1875), p. 392.

20. Johann Christoph Blumhardt, *Blätter aus Bad Boll* (1876), pp. 137–138.

21. Johann Christoph Blumhardt, *Vom Glauben bis ans Ende* (Berlin, 1926), p. 17.

22. Johann Christoph Blumhardt, *Blätter aus Bad Boll* (1876), p. 120.

23. *Ibid.*, p. 152.

24. *Ibid.*, p. 192.

25. Christoph Friedrich Blumhardt, *Sterbet, so wird Jesus leben! Predigten und Andachten aus den Jahren 1888 bis 1896*, ed. R. Lejeune (Zürich and Leipzig, 1925), extracts from pp. 156–158.

26. Christoph Friedrich Blumhardt, *Ihr Menschen seid Gottes!*, p. 429.

27. *Ibid.*, pp. 312, 313.

28. Christoph Friedrich Blumhardt, *Der zwölfjährige Jesus im Tempel*, unpublished sermon, January 12, 1913.

29. Johann Christoph Blumhardt, *Gesammelte Werke, 2. Band: Evangelien-Predigten* (Karlsruhe, 1887), extracts from pp. 70–78.

30. Christoph Friedrich Blumhardt, *Sterbet, so wird Jesus leben*, p. 155.

31. Christoph Friedrich Blumhardt, *Lasset die Kindlein zu mir kommen!* (Stuttgart, 1910), published sermon, January 9, 1910, pp. 3–4.

32. Christoph Friedrich Blumhardt, *Ihr Menschen seid Gottes!*, pp. 427–428.

33. Christoph Friedrich Blumhardt, *Sterbet, so wird Jesus leben*, pp. 155–156.

34. *Ibid.*, pp. 154–155.

35. Christoph Friedrich Blumhardt, *Lasset die Kindlein zu mir kommen!*, pp. 4–5.

36. Christoph Friedrich Blumhardt, *Sterbet, so wird Jesus leben*, p. 155.

37. Christoph Friedrich Blumhardt, *Lasset die Kindlein zu mir kommen!*, pp. 5–6.

For more information visit **www.plough.com.**

Or write:

Plough Publishing House
1-800-521-8011 ● 845-572-3455
PO BOX 398 ● Walden, NY 12586 ● USA
Brightling Rd ● Robertsbridge ● East Sussex TN32 5DR ● UK
4188 Gwydir Highway ● Elsmore, NSW 2360 ● Australia